ABUNDANT TRUTH INTERNATIONAL MINISTRIES

Abundant Truth Leadership Series

Keys to Pastoral Ministry and Recovery

Help for Wounded Healers

Roderick Levi Evans

Keys to Pastoral Ministry and Recovery
Help for Wounded Healers

All Rights Reserved. © 2004 Roderick L. Evans

No part of this book may be reproduced or transmitted in any form or by any means, graphic, electronic, or mechanical, including photocopying, recording, taping or by any information storage or retrieval system, without the permission in writing from the publisher.

Front & Back Cover Designs by Abundant Truth International Publishing
Image by Leandro De Carvalho from Pixabay

Abundant Truth Publishing
an imprint of Abundant Truth International Ministries

For information address:
Abundant Truth International
P.O. Box 126
Camden, NC 27921

I ISBN: 978-1-60141-610-0

Printed in the United States of America

Unless otherwise indicated, all of the scripture quotations are taken from the *Authorized King James Version* of the Bible. Scripture quotations marked with NIV are taken from the *New International Version* of the Bible. Scripture quotations marked with NASV are taken from the *New American Standard Version* of the Bible. Scripture quotations marked with Amplified are taken from the *Amplified Bible*.

Contents

Introduction

Chapter 1 - Prologue: 1
The Lysterian Legacy

Deification of Leaders   5
Reluctancy of Leaders   7

Chapter 2 - The Davidic   13
Dilemma

Emotional Influences   20
Social Influences   24

CONTENTS (cont.)

Chapter 3 – The Recovery of Manasseh   **29**

Humility   *36*

Overcome Fear   *38*

Ask   *39*

Listen/follow Through   *40*

Accountability   *42*

Chapter 4 – Creating an Atmosphere   **45**

Messages of Love   *49*

Motivate the leaders   *51*

CONTENTS (cont.)

Mobilize the Masses   52

Bibliography   57

Introduction

God anoints and endows individuals with gifts and talents to serve in the Church. However, some have missed the very purpose of gifts and ministries in the Church. In the Abundant Truth Leadership Series, we will endeavor to present a proper foundation for believers to minister upon.

In this publication

In this issue, we want to examine the influences surrounding this problem in leadership. We will discuss the reasons why pastors and leaders do not receive needed ministry. In addition, we will explore steps that leaders can employ to receive the help that they need.

It is our prayer that those who minister will be blessed and strengthened from the information presented.

-Chapter 1-

PROLOGUE:
The Lysterian Legacy

"We also are men of like passions with you and preach unto you that ye should turn from these vanities unto the living God." (Acts 14:15)

After a man of Lystra received healing, the people wanted to worship the apostles, Paul and Barnabas, and offer sacrifices to them. Barnabas and Paul said,

> *"We also are men of like passions with you and preach unto you that ye should turn from these vanities unto the living God." (Acts 14:15)*

Deification of Leaders

This same scenario is demonstrated even in today's churches. Parishioners deify pastors and church leaders. They hear them present powerful and stirring messages about Jesus Christ and the Christian Faith. The church leaders, to them, seemingly are unaffected by the

evils of today.

Therefore, some believe that pastors and other leaders have moved beyond this world and its problems. However, this is simply not true. In spite of publicized church scandals involving clergy, pastors and leaders are still expected to be perfect and without issues.

It then becomes difficult for a pastor or leader with sins, weaknesses, and problems to receive help. In addition, past scandals involving well-known ministers and denominations have only managed to create fear among leaders.

Reluctancy of Leaders

As a result, many leaders will not seek help without the fear of negative repercussions. However, scandals of the past and present should provoke a pursuit of accountability, integrity, and purity among the clergy. Pastors and other leaders need assistance, as does every Christian.

Parishioners have to understand that their leaders are human while understanding that the calling upon their lives demands a greater level of sacrifice and service. If parishioners have problems and struggles, their leaders will have them also.

However, pastors and leaders have to overcome internal and external influences if they are to receive assistance.

Notes:

-Chapter 2-

The David Dilema

The woman conceived and sent word to David, saying, "I am pregnant."

(II Samuel 11:5 NIV)

In the book of 2 Samuel, chapter 11, the account of David's adultery with Bathsheba is recorded. In this well-known story, we see that David was in a dilemma as to what he should do after discovering that Bathsheba was pregnant.

The woman conceived and sent word to David, saying, "I am pregnant." (II Samuel 11:5 NIV)

David's dilemma led him to make the horrific choice of devising a scheme to kill Bathsheba's husband to cover his sin. The Bible does not tell us specifically why David chose this extreme course of action.

He knew that God was merciful and would not leave him. However, due to his personal motivations, he would not simply face his sin, but multiplied it.

If he had sought true forgiveness from the Lord and faced the consequences of his actions, his godly legacy may have been spotted by adultery, but not compounded by deceit, scheming, and abuse of power to commit murder.

Pastors and leaders today are faced with a dilemma as to how should they receive help for public and personal downfalls, mistakes, and sins. David did not seek help, but the modern pastor and leader should not follow David's legacy.

Again, though David's personal motivations were not elucidated, we will not look at reasons why today's leaders do not receive help, which could lead to greater sin and downfall.

Reasons Why Leaders Don't Receive Help

The most common factors that hinder leaders. from receiving help are pride, embarrassment, hopelessness, ministry security, and family.

These influences can be placed in two categories: Emotional and Social. Until these influences are removed, leaders will continue to minister while they need ministry.

Emotional Influences

Pride. Pastors and leaders are

afraid to appear vulnerable, less spiritual, or "human." They will not admit that they have a problem because they are supposed to lead. Therefore, leaders believe that to display any signs of imperfection indicate a lack of spirituality or maturity to other clergy or laity.

Embarrassment. Fear and feelings of embarrassment have the ability to the pursuit for assistance. If the sin is considered highly immoral, leaders are liable to be selective about what they share. Embarrassment grips the mind and heart producing paranoia and guilt as they share feelings.

In turn, personal feelings of embarrassment are transferred onto others. So that, when they speak to anyone concerning their problems, any reaction perceived to be negative or judgmental will stop the quest for help.

Hopelessness. Hopelessness is the silent prison that takes certain leaders captive. They preach and give advice, even though they have lost hope in God and themselves. They minister out of routine, not expecting any results in their own personal lives.

Some ministers develop the attitude, "I am a minister, I should have the answer for my own problems," or "I have tried all that I know and it has not worked."

Therefore, depression, guilt, and unbelief seize their emotions producing doubt. They began to descend into the pit of hopelessness. In this mindset, the reception of counsel and support is frustrated.

Social Influences

Now we will turn attention to the social influences which hinder pastors and leaders from seeking and receiving help.

Security. Some pastors and leaders do not admit they need help for ministry security. Various religious organizations choose their ministers by the vote or interview rather than by the appointment of denominational leaders.

Leaders are chosen by perception rather than reality. Therefore, they feel pressured into keeping personal issues hidden for fear of losing an appointment or position. Though the Church is supposed to offer forgiveness and restoration, the unfortunate truth is that good leaders have been rejected after confessing personal struggles.

Family. One final reason that pastors and leaders do not seek for help is family. Leaders need the comfort of confidentially when resolving hidden issues. Because of their positions, leaders are concerned about their problems being revealed publicly.

The strain that it could bring upon family relations could be seemingly irreversible. Thus, leaders choose to deal with their issues alone to spare their family from undue embarrassment, shame, or break up.

Notes:

-Chapter 3-

The Recovery of Manasseh

And prayed unto him: and he was intreated of him (the Lord), and heard his supplication, and brought him again to Jerusalem into his kingdom. Then **Manasseh** *knew that the LORD he was God.* ***(2 Chronicles 33:13 NIV*** *Parenthesis mine)*

In the book of 2 Kings, chapter 33, we read of Manasseh becoming king, and how he led the nation in debauchery and wickedness. God allowed Manasseh to be taken prisoner by his enemies.

However, while imprisoned due to the consequences of his rebellion against God, Manasseh sought recovery through prayer. God head him and restored him to his throne.

And prayed unto him: and he was intreated of him (the Lord), *and heard his supplication, and brought him again to Jerusalem into his kingdom. Then **Manasseh** knew that the LORD he was God. (2 Chronicles 33:13 NIV Parenthesis mine)*

Steps for Pastors/Leaders

Manasseh's story reveals that there is recovery even after a fall. God heard Manasseh after he took the first step in seeking after God.

Pastors and leaders today also can take certain steps to recover after a fall.

Pride, embarrassment, security, hopelessness and, and family are the major reasons among many why pastors and leaders continue to minister and counsel without receiving ministry. However, these two questions remain:

1. *"How can leaders find counsel and support for the issues in their lives?"*

2. *"How can pastors make their congregations a place of*

ministry and restoration for their parishioners?"

There are certain keys that pastors and leaders must use in order to unlock the door to freedom from issues.

Humility

Leaders have to be willing to admit there is a problem. The scriptures say that confession is made unto salvation (Romans 10:10).

Before Christ is received, sin and guilt before God has to be acknowledged. It is then that one can receive Him. Likewise, leaders have to humble themselves (like Manasseh) and admit the truth about themselves and their situations.

It is unprofitable to rationalize sin and weakness. Humility demands honesty within and to God. God will supply grace to those who are humble.

But he giveth more grace. Wherefore he saith, God resisteth the proud, but giveth grace unto the humble. (James 4:6)

Overcome Fear

Humility is the beginning. However, admittance without action is useless. Once confession is made, the next step is to overcome fear. Four out of the five reasons for pastors and leaders not receiving help are the offspring of fear.

Whatever fears may be present, leaders must take control. Fears have to be presented at the foot of the cross. Pastors and leaders have to remember that God has not given us the spirit of fear. Fear has to be dispelled.

For God hath not given us the spirit of fear; but of power, and of love, and of a sound mind. (2 Timothy 1:7)

Ask

The Bible says that you have not, because you do not ask (James 4:2b). After humbling themselves and overcoming fears, leaders have to ask for help. Though leaders may have to be selective, it should not deter them from seeking guidance.

There are ministries designed to aid pastors and leaders. If pastors feel they cannot receive the best help possible from within, then they have to seek help from outside sources.

A little research is needed depending on the need, but help is available. Again, leaders must be willing to admit their problems and ask for help.

Listen/Follow Through

Pastors and leaders understand that information without application is useless. Once counsel is received, leaders have to follow the directives given to them.

> *But be ye doers of the word, and not hearers only, deceiving your own selves. (James 1:22)*

Leaders have to resist a "know it all" mentality. Pastors and leaders are accustomed to dispensing advice, but they have to know how to take it. Proverbs tells us that wise men hear. Leaders who truly want help will listen and take action.

Accountability

After receiving counsel, pastors and leaders should submit to some form of accountability. It is imperative to have individuals that they can confide in.

In addition, leaders can benefit from persons who challenge them in their walk with God and their ministries. Accountability is a necessary precaution, so that they can maintain a life of purity and integrity.

Notes:

-Chapter 4-

Creating an Atmosphere

The pastor must hold to principles of holy living through love.

Since pastors have the oversight of numerous people, they have the ability to transform their congregations into places of God's healing and restoration for parishioners who have secret struggles. This can be done in a practical manner.

Messages of Love

First, pastors may preach and teach messages whose central themes are love, deliverance, forgiveness, accountability, and restoration for a prescribed length of time.

The messages should be forthright. The pastor must hold to principles of holy living through love. In this way the believer can be reminded that part of the new birth is the ability to overcome personal sins and weakness.

It does demand discipline, but through the help of the indwelling Spirit, and the support of others, recovery remains a stabilizing influence in the believer's heart and mind.

Motivate the Leaders

Second, pastors may hold private sessions with other leaders in the congregation. The focus on these meetings is to create, first, an atmosphere among the leaders whereby they can feel secure in the love and support of one another. The result should be a system of accountability among the leaders.

Third, pastors should instruct these leaders on how to implement teachings and programs around themes of love, acceptance, forgiveness, and restoration in Christ.

Mobilize the Masses

Bible study, youth groups, and Sunday school class instructors will promote this theme in these settings. In this manner, the whole congregation will be involved in the healing and restoration of one another.

Pastors and leaders are placed in the Body of Christ to help men and women overcome and cope with the struggles of life. Their ministries are less effective when they have unresolved issues.

Clergy and laity have to relieve leaders of undue pressure, so that they can receive ministry. In turn, they will able to fulfill their God-given ministries without hindrances from personal issues.

In addition, pastors should shape their local assemblies into places where individuals are given the opportunity to receive forgiveness and counsel without reproach. The result is a vibrant, healthy church.

Notes:

KEYS TO PASTORAL MINISTRY AND RECOVERY
Help for Wounded Healers

Bibliography

Smith, William. *Smith's Bible Dictionary.* Holman Bible Publishers. Nashville, Tennessee. c1994

The Bible Library. *The Bible Library CD Rom Disc.* Ellis Enterprises Incorporated, (c)1988 – 2000. 4205 McAuley Blvd., Suite 385, Oklahoma City, OK 73120. All Rights Reserved.

Lockman Foundation. *Comparative Study Bible.* Zondervan Publishing House. Grand Rapids, MI, c1984

Notes:

Notes:

KEYS TO PASTORAL MINISTRY AND RECOVERY
Help for Wounded Healers

Notes:

Notes:

KEYS TO PASTORAL MINISTRY AND RECOVERY
Help for Wounded Healers

www.ingramcontent.com/pod-product-compliance
Lightning Source LLC
Chambersburg PA
CBHW050344010526
44119CB00049B/686